RESEARCH DISCOVERY GUIDE

SIGNIFICANT PEOPLE FROM HISTORY

Jackie Robinson

BASED ON THE BOOK
Who Was Jackie Robinson?
by Gail Herman

Guide Written by Liam Bredberg

blackbird&company
EDUCATIONAL PRESS

Visit us at

blackbirdandcompany.com

Explore our full range of Discovery guides:

Hatchling: Reading | Writing | Phonics

Earlybird: Literature & Writing

Literature & Writing

Storymaker

One True Sentence

Operation Lexicon

Intro to Composition

Exploring Poetry

Research Science

Research History

Copyright © 2020 by Blackbird & Company Educational Press.

All rights reserved. No part of this book may be reproduced or utilized in any form or by any electronic or mechanical means, including photocopying, without permission in writing from the publisher except for the use of brief quotations in a book review.

Printed in the U.S.A.

First Printing, 2020

ISBN 978-1-953357-19-9

V1 01 Sep 2020

SKU: 20-57199

www.blackbirdandcompany.com

Table of Contents

Introduction .... **v**
    How This Guide is Organized .... **viii**
    Writing Guidelines .... **x**
    Grading Guidelines .... **xiv**

Let's Get Started **1**

Section 1 .... **5**

Section 2 .... **15**

Section 3 .... **25**

Section 4 .... **35**

Section 5 .... **45**

Introduction

What's in a name? The history of the human race is in names. Our objective friends do not understand that, since they move in a world of objects which can be counted and numbered. They reduce the great names of the past to dust and ashes. This they call scientific history. But the whole meaning of history is in the proof that there have lived people before the present time whom it is important to meet.

Eugen Rosenstock-Huessy

How This Guide is Organized

Guide Sections - *overview*

This guide is divided into 5 weekly sections:

SECTIONS 1-3

The first three sections each cover a period of the individual's life through the following elements:

Reading
» Weekly reading assignment to begin each section.

Character Lexicon
» Character traits to define and use in original sentences.

Comprehension
» Questions to reinforce observation and understanding.

Writing (BODY – 1st DRAFT)
» Structured paragraphs to begin building the body of the essay.

SECTION 4

Writing (OPENING/CLOSING – 1st DRAFT)
» Structured paragraphs to open and close the essay.

Writing (COMPLETED ESSAY – FINAL DRAFT)
» Combine opening, closing, and body to form the complete essay.

SECTION 5

Culminating Project
» Ideas to further explore and creatively express related topics.

✱ SUPPLEMENTAL READING

The included supplemental reading can be done at anytime along the way. Encourage students to read all they can to help give a fuller picture of the people they are learning about.

How This Guide is Organized (cont.)

Guide Sections - *details*

Assignment Checklist

This form is to be used by both the student and the teacher. Encourage your student to utilize this as a time management device and have them mark off each element as it is completed. The teacher can then comment, evaluate, and grade each element. Depending on the student's learning style and classroom logistics, each element can be evaluated individually or each section can be evaluated when all its elements are complete. On the following pages we have included sample grading and writing guidelines to assist you.

Reading

These research guides are designed to explore the life of a real person. When exploring non-fiction information it is important to seek out multiple sources. We have provided a core and a supplemental reading source for this purpose. Supplemental reading can often be completed in one sitting. Longer supplemental reading should be paced parallel to core reading. This reading provides additional details students can utilize in their essays. We understand that people read, experience, and absorb stories in many different ways and at different rates. However, we recommend students read through each assignment in one sitting before moving on. Keeping the flow of a story intact should be a priority. Therefore, we encourage students to set aside a substantial block of time for reading each week.

Character Lexicon

Exploring and describing the traits of the character is the first element encountered in the guide after reading. This element is the preliminary research that will contribute to the crafting of an original essay. It is designed to help students develop impressions and opinions as they explore traits that each of these remarkable men and women from history possess. As students define and consider the vocabulary words, they will discover a lexicon of traits unique to each of these exemplary individuals. Students will then apply and utilize the lexicon to communicate, through an essay, what they have discovered.

Comprehension

Following the *Character Lexicon* section is a series of questions that will help students engage in the art of crafting complex sentences as they gather specific details of each character's life. Answering questions in complete sentences is good practice, as it reinforces clear thinking and writing skills. It may be helpful for some students to survey the questions before beginning the reading assignment, however, they should not be answered until the reading assignment has been completed so as to maintain continuity while reading. Encouraging students to refer to the book and to note page numbers as they complete the *Comprehension* section is a useful research skill, especially if the guide is used in group settings where information will be discussed.

Writing

The writing assignment is intended to make the reader think, respond and apply, with the added challenge of producing a well crafted, articulate answer. More specifically, this element consists of a directed writing assignment that will culminate in a biographical essay. Beginning with topic wheels to help students organize information gleaned during research, the writing element will guide them through all the stages of the process necessary to craft a unique communication of the historical figure.

This element introduces and reinforces the process of writing, helping students to transform abstract thoughts and ideas into tangible words, sentences, and paragraphs. Writing a rough draft is the first step in completing the assignment. The student should then self-edit the rough draft as much as possible with the usual checks for spelling, grammar, and punctuation, while also paying attention to readability, clarity, and creativity. The student should also conference with their teacher at this time. In *Section 4*, the rough drafts will be combined and rewritten as the final draft, incorporating all edits for a clean and polished essay.

Culminating Project

The creative project should be inspired by something that sparked interest or excited you. Use this opportunity to create something tangible and memorable from the reading that will inspire others.

Writing Guidelines

Five Elements of the Essay - *overview*

Each completed essay will include the following:

1. **Opening Paragraph** (WRITTEN IN SECTION 4)
   » Open your essay with a *Hook*, a *Context Sentence*, and a *Thesis Statement*.

2. **Topic Paragraph 1** (WRITTEN IN SECTION 1)
   » An expanded paragraph developed from *Topic Wheel 1*.

3. **Topic Paragraph 2** (WRITTEN IN SECTION 2)
   » An expanded paragraph developed from *Topic Wheel 2*.

4. **Topic Paragraph 3** (WRITTEN IN SECTION 3)
   » An expanded paragraph developed from *Topic Wheel 3*.

5. **Closing Paragraph** (WRITTEN IN SECTION 4)
   » Close your essay with a *Weave*, an *Echo*, and a *Twist*.

Writing Guidelines (cont.)

Five Elements of the Essay - *details*

1. Opening Paragraph:

Hook
The *Hook* is the first sentence of your essay, the singular sentence that will grab your reader's attention.

Context Sentence
The *Context Sentence* is the sentence that moves the reader from the *Hook* to the *Thesis*.

Thesis Statement
The *Thesis Statement* is a single sentence that introduces readers to the main ideas of your research.

Example Opening Paragraph (writing about Louisa May Alcott)

(Hook) *Little Women* might be the first thought that comes to mind when asked about author Louisa May Alcott, but when it comes to considering her life, there was nothing little about this woman.

(Context) This was a writer who brought a diverse experience to her stories, having been a servant, a seamstress, and a Civil War nurse.

(Thesis) Lousia May Alcott wrote what she knew, and her wonderful stories weave together history and her personal experience, capturing the imagination of readers.

2—4. Topic Paragraphs

Topic Wheel
Topic Wheels help you organize your thoughts and focus on significant details that you wish to communicate. First *Brainstorm* single words or short phrases that might work for the *Topic Wheel*, then complete each spoke of the *Topic Wheel* by choosing the best ideas that describe, expand, and add interest to your topic. Each spoke will be the foundation of one complete sentence. Together, all of the spokes will form the supporting sentences of your *Topic Paragraph*.

5. Closing Paragraph

Weave
The *Weave* is the first sentence of your closing paragraph. This is the sentence that will help your reader begin to come to a close.

Echo
The *Echo* is the sentence that moves the reader from the *Weave* to the *Twist*.

Twist
The *Twist* is a single sentence that closes your essay and leaves readers with an idea that will keep them thinking on your topic.

Example Closing Paragraph

(Weave) Considering the fact that Louisa May Alcott lived nearly 200 years ago, in a specific time and place, it is remarkable that her writing is so engaging to a diverse audience.

(Echo) This woman was a remarkable writer.

(Twist) Lousia May Alcott was not a little woman, but rather a woman with big ideas.

Writing Guidelines (cont.)

Five Stages of the Writing Process - *overview*

As you write, keep in mind the 5 steps that lead to excellent work:

1. **Topic Brainstorm**
   » Think about it. Come up with great ideas for your Topic Wheel.
2. **First Draft**
   » Get your thoughts organized and on paper.
3. **Conference**
   » Carefully read your first draft, have someone else read it and offer input.
4. **Edit/Polish**
   » Check spelling, grammar, content, and style. Make desired changes.
5. **Final Draft**
   » Copy your work using your best penmanship.

Writing Guidelines (cont.)

Five Stages of the Writing Process - *details*

1. Brainstorm

As you Brainstorm and complete your Topic Wheels, use the opportunity to plan how you will engage your readers. Think about the famous person you are writing about and imagine them as a real person. What was their day-to-day life like? What brought him or her joy? What did he or she look forward to? What things made life difficult? What made life fun? Write down as many ideas related to the topic as you can think of, then choose your five best ideas to complete your Topic Wheel.

2. First Draft

Use your completed topic wheels as a scaffolding to develop a first draft of each Topic Paragraph. Be sure to open each of the expanded paragraphs with an interesting topic sentence that introduces the reader to the paragraph's topic. Present your ideas in a sequence that is logical. Finally, at the end of your paragraph, craft a single closing sentence that will leave your reader with an idea to continue thinking about.

When you have completed the first draft of your Topic Paragraphs, develop the first draft of your opening and closing paragraphs in a similar way.

Remember, the best way to get your First Draft started is to JUST START WRITING! Even if it's not exactly what you want to say, words on paper are much easier to edit than words that are stuck in your head.

3. Conference

Now that you have the First Draft of your complete essay, an Opening Paragraph, three Topic Paragraphs, and a Closing Paragraph, make a careful check of spelling and grammar, and then get a second opinion. Having someone else read your essay before it is done is an excellent way to find out how well you are communicating your ideas and if you are capturing the reader's interest.

4. Edit/Polish

After conferencing, be open to input and decide how you want to incorporate any comments from your reader. Make your changes and read your essay again, out loud if possible. While reading, check your spelling and grammar one more time and make any needed changes.

5. Final Draft

So far, you have Brainstormed, Drafted, Conferenced, and Polished. The hard work is done! Now re-write your essay using your best penmanship and make it beautiful for others to see. Even if you don't think your writing is great, this will be great practice, and others will appreciate the effort and care that you put into your work.

Grading Guidelines

Full points are awarded for complete and creative work that goes beyond the basic requirements. No points are awarded when the work has not been done. Know your student and individualize the following grading guidelines by awarding points accordingly.

Reading	5 Points
Character Lexicon	5 Points
Comprehension	5 Points
Writing	10 Points (See below)
Total	25 Points

Grading Your Student's Writing
When evaluating your student's writing, use the following guidelines:

Accomplished ....(10 points)
> Creatively focuses on the topic
> Uses logical progression of ideas to develop and supports topic with details
> Varies sentence structure
> Uses interesting transitions and strong word choice
> Mature understanding of writing conventions

Proficient ....(8 points)
> Focuses on topic and includes adequate support
> Uses logical progression of ideas to develop and loosely supports topic
> Some varied sentence structure
> Transitions and word choice are adequate but not creative
> General understanding of writing conventions

Basic ....(6 points)
> Topic is addressed, but unclear
> Lacks logical progression of ideas and support is weak
> Sentences are stagnant and uninteresting
> Lack of transitions and average word choice
> Partial understanding of writing conventions

Limited ....(4 points)
> Topic may be mentioned, but not clearly addressed and supported loosely
> Organization pattern is weak
> Writing contains sentence fragments and run-on's
> Poor transitions and word choice
> Definite misunderstanding of writing conventions

Poor ....(2 points)
> Topic is not addressed or clearly supported
> Organizational pattern is lacking
> Sentence structure is insufficient
> Non-existent transitions and inappropriate word choice
> Frequent errors in basic writing conventions

Let's Get Started

Jackie Robinson | **Get Started**

Assignment Checklist

Reading assignments: ***Who Was Jackie Robinson?***

Supplemental Reading: ***A Picture Book of Jackie Robinson*** — by David A. Adler

ASSIGNMENT	POINTS	TEACHER COMMENTS	GRADE

Section 1: *Who Was Jackie Robinson? — Chapter 5: Ready for Change*

- ○ Reading ___ /5
- ○ Character Lexicon ___ /5
- ○ Comprehension ___ /5
- ○ Writing (10 possible)
  - ○ Brainstorm ___ /3
  - ○ Topic Wheel ___ /3
  - ○ First Draft ___ /4

___ /25

Section 2: *Chapters 6: Army Days — Chapter 9: Spring Training*

- ○ Reading ___ /5
- ○ Character Lexicon ___ /5
- ○ Comprehension ___ /5
- ○ Writing (10 possible)
  - ○ Brainstorm ___ /3
  - ○ Topic Wheel ___ /3
  - ○ First Draft ___ /4

___ /25

Section 3: *Chapters 10: The Minors — Chapter 15: The Legend Lives On*

- ○ Reading ___ /5
- ○ Character Lexicon ___ /5
- ○ Comprehension ___ /5
- ○ Writing (10 possible)
  - ○ Brainstorm ___ /3
  - ○ Topic Wheel ___ /3
  - ○ First Draft ___ /4

___ /25

Section 4: *Opening — Closing — Final Draft*

- ○ Opening First Draft ___ /5
- ○ Closing First Draft ___ /5
- ○ Final Draft ___ /15

___ /25

Final Score ___ /100

Essay Diagram

Use this diagram to help you pace your essay.

Section 1-3: Write the first drafts of your 3 Topic Paragraphs.

Section 4: Write the first drafts of your opening and closing paragraphs. Compile your 5 paragraphs into your final essay.

opening

Your 3 sentence opening will include:
- **Hook**
- **Context**
- **Thesis**

topic 1: Early Life.

topic 2: Life's Work

topic 3: Later Life and Legacy

closing

Your 3 sentence closing will include:
- **Weave**
- **Echo**
- **Twist**

Section 1 » Early Life

Read » Who Was Jackie Robinson?—Chapter 5

CHARACTER LEXICON

Character Lexicon > Definitions

Use a dictionary to define the following character traits:

| loving | athletic | shy | bright | selfless |

1.

2.

3.

4.

5.

Character Lexicon > Sentences

Use each character trait in a complete and original sentence about the person you are studying. Use your definitions and be sure to incorporate specific details from the reading.

1.

2.

3.

4.

5.

COMPREHENSION   Jackie Robinson | **Section 1**

Comprehension Questions

Answer the following questions using complete sentences.

1. How old was Jackie Robinson when he was entered into the Baseball Hall of Fame?

2. Why didn't Jackie want his plaque in the Hall of Fame to mention him being the first African American player in major league baseball?

3. Why did the school kids always want Jackie on their sports teams?

4. What sports did Jackie play in high school?

5. What did Rachel Isum assume about Jackie before she met him?

6. How did Rachel's opinion of Jackie change after she got to know him?

7. What happened in Hawaii when Jackie was travelling back to California?

topic 1

begin topic paragraph 1 »

WRITING   Jackie Robinson | Section 1

Writing > Brainstorm

Use this page to write down words or phrases that support **Topic 1** on the next page.

How many ideas can you think of?

Topic 1:

1.
2.
3.
4.
5.
6.
7.
8.
9.
10.

WRITING • Jackie Robinson | **Section 1**

Writing > Topic Wheel 1

Use this topic wheel to help you plan **Topic Paragraph 1**.

Choose the five best ideas from your brainstorm on the previous page and write each into one of the spokes below.

Each spoke will be made into one complete sentence of **Topic Paragraph 1**.

topic 1

TOPIC 1

Early Life

1.
2.
3.
4.
5.

WRITING

Writing > Topic Paragraph 1: First Draft

1. Begin your paragraph with an opening sentence that introduces your subject.
2. Use the five ideas from **Topic Wheel 1** to create the five main sentences of your paragraph.
3. Close your paragraph with a strong clincher.

Conference, edit, and *polish* your First Draft in this section.

Complete the Final Draft in Section 4.

1. Opening sentence

2. Body sentences

Writing > Topic Paragraph 1: First Draft (cont.)

3. Closing sentence

Section 2 » Life's Work

Read » Chapters 6 — 9

Character Lexicon > Definitions

Use a dictionary to define the following character traits:

| daring | lonely | fed-up | nervous | proud |

1.

2.

3.

4.

5.

Character Lexicon > Sentences

Use each character trait in a complete and original sentence about the person you are studying. Use your definitions and be sure to incorporate specific details from the reading.

1.

2.

3.

4.

5.

COMPREHENSION Jackie Robinson | **Section 2**

Comprehension Questions

Answer the following questions using complete sentences.

1. Why was Jackie put on trial when he was in the military?

2. Why did Jackie choose to play baseball when football was the sport he loved the most?

3. Why was life in the Negro League hard for Jackie?

4. Why did Branch Rickey bring Jackie to the Brooklyn Dodgers' office?

5. Which minor league team did Jackie play for before he was promoted to play for the Dodgers?

6. How long did it take for Jackie and Rachel to make it to Florida for spring training?

7. Why was the clubhouse so crowded after Jackie's first game?

topic 2

begin topic paragraph 2 »

WRITING

Writing > Brainstorm

Use this page to write down words or phrases that support **Topic 2** on the next page.

How many ideas can you think of?

Topic 2:

1.
2.
3.
4.
5.
6.
7.
8.
9.
10.

WRITING

Writing > Topic Wheel 2

Use this topic wheel to help you plan **Topic Paragraph 2**.

Choose the five best ideas from your brainstorm on the previous page and write each into one of the spokes below.

Each spoke will be made into one complete sentence of **Topic Paragraph 2**.

topic 2

TOPIC 2
Life's Work

1.
2.
3.
4.
5.

WRITING

Writing > Topic Paragraph 1: First Draft

1. Begin your paragraph with an opening sentence that introduces your subject.
2. Use the five ideas from **Topic Wheel 2** to create the five main sentences of your paragraph.
3. Close your paragraph with a strong clincher.

> *Conference, edit,* and *polish* your First Draft in this section.
>
> Complete the Final Draft in Section 4.

1. Opening sentence

2. Body sentences

Writing > Topic Paragraph 2: First Draft (cont.)

3. Closing sentence

Section 3 » **Later Life and Legacy**

Read » Chapters 10 — 15

Character Lexicon > Definitions

Use a dictionary to define the following character traits:

| generous | devoted | busy | legendary | peaceful |

1.

2.

3.

4.

5.

Character Lexicon > Sentences

Use each character trait in a complete and original sentence about the person you are studying. Use your definitions and be sure to incorporate specific details from the reading.

1.

2.

3.

4.

5.

COMPREHENSION   Jackie Robinson | **Section 3**

Comprehension Questions

Answer the following questions using complete sentences.

1. Why did Jackie and Rachel like living in Montreal?

2. How did Leo Durocher persuade his players to let Jackie play for the Dodgers?

3. Why was Jackie disappointed when the Dodgers won in his first game?

4. What did Pee Wee Reese do when the crowd told him to stop playing with Jackie?

5. What did Time Magazine name Jackie?

6. What was the amazing thing that happened in game 1 of the World Series?

7. What did Jackie do when he worked for the NAACP?

topic 3

begin topic paragraph 3 »

Writing > Brainstorm

Use this page to write down words or phrases that support **Topic 3** on the next page.

How many ideas can you think of?

Topic 3: _____

1. _____
2. _____
3. _____
4. _____
5. _____
6. _____
7. _____
8. _____
9. _____
10. _____

WRITING　　　　　　　　　　　　　　　　　　　　　　　　　　　　　Jackie Robinson | **Section 3**

Writing > Topic Wheel 3

Use this topic wheel to help you plan **Topic Paragraph 3**.

Choose the five best ideas from your brainstorm on the previous page and write each into one of the spokes below.

Each spoke will be made into one complete sentence of **Topic Paragraph 3**.

topic 3

TOPIC 3

Later Life and Legacy

1.
2.
3.
4.
5.

WRITING

Writing > Topic Paragraph 3: First Draft

1. Begin your paragraph with an opening sentence that introduces your subject.
2. Use the five ideas from **Topic Wheel 3** to create the five main sentences of your paragraph.
3. Close your paragraph with a strong clincher.

Conference, edit, and *polish* your First Draft in this section.

Complete the Final Draft in Section 4.

1. Opening sentence

2. Body sentences

Writing > Topic Paragraph 3: First Draft (cont.)

3. Closing sentence

Section 4 » **Final Essay**

Writing > Final Essay

Congratulations!
You've done the hard work of writing the core content of your essay.

On the following pages:

1. » **Write your 3 sentence opening paragraph**
After writing the first draft of your opening paragraph begin the first draft of your closing paragraph.

2. » **Write your 3 sentence closing paragraph**
After writing the first draft of your closing paragraph conference, edit, and polish both your opening and closing paragraphs, then move on to the final step.

3. » **Bring all the pieces together**
Combine your opening paragraph, your 3 topic paragraphs, and your closing paragraph into one final essay.

Writing > Opening Paragraph: First Draft

1. Begin your Opening Paragraph with a **Hook** that grabs the reader's attention.
2. Use a **Context Sentence** to move to the **Thesis**.
3. Close your paragraph with a **Thesis** that introduces your main idea .

Writing > Closing Paragraph: First Draft

1. Begin your Closing Paragraph with a **Weave** that begins to close your essay.
2. Use an **Echo** to move your reader to the **Twist**.
3. Close your paragraph with a **Twist** that will keep your readers thinking.

Writing > Final Draft

Once you have **conferenced**, **edited**, and **polished** your 5 paragraphs, *opening – topic 1 – topic 2 – topic 3 – closing,* complete your final draft by combining them here, in the correct order, using your best penmanship.

Writing > Final Draft (cont.)

Writing > Final Draft (cont.)

Writing > Final Draft (cont.)

Section 5 » **Final Project**

Assignment Options

Following are suggestions for creative projects and further research:

1. What is your favorite thing you learned about Jackie Robinson? Create a diorama inspired by it.

2. Research and draw pictures of all the different uniforms Jackie wore throughout college, the minor leagues, and the major leagues.

3. Research a few more of the first African American players that broke color barriers in major sports. Write a short research paper and present it to your class or family.

4. Jackie moved around the country a lot during his life. Look at the timeline in the back of the book and create a map of the country showing all the places that Jackie lived and played baseball.

5. Write a short paper about the Civil Rights Movement. Who were the most important figures and what were they fighting for? When did it occur? What did it accomplish? Present your research to your class or family.

Need a little inspiration?

Scan here to view our student project gallery!